My Little Golden Book About

Johnny Appleseed

By Lori Haskins Houran
Illustrated by Geneviève Godbout

The editors would like to thank Cheryl Ogden, Museum Director,
The Johnny Appleseed Educational Center & Museum, Urbana University, Urbana, Ohio,
for her assistance in the preparation of this book.

A GOLDEN BOOK • NEW YORK

Text copyright © 2017 by Lori Haskins Houran
Illustrations copyright © 2017 by Geneviève Godbout
All rights reserved. Published in the United States by Golden Books, an imprint of
Random House Children's Books, a division of Penguin Random House LLC, 1745 Broadway,
New York, NY 10019, and in Canada by Penguin Random House Canada Limited, Toronto.
Golden Books, A Golden Book, A Little Golden Book, the G colophon, and the distinctive gold
spine are registered trademarks of Penguin Random House LLC.
randomhousekids.com
Educators and librarians, for a variety of teaching tools, visit us at
RHTeachersLibrarians.com
Library of Congress Control Number: 2015956503
ISBN 978-0-399-55590-9 (trade) — ISBN 978-0-399-55591-6 (ebook)
Printed in the United States of America
10 9 8 7 6

On a fine September day more than two hundred years ago, a boy named John Chapman was born.

Someday he would be famous! But he would be known by a different name: Johnny Appleseed.

Johnny grew up in Massachusetts,
in a small, crowded house.

He liked to take long walks in the woods, where
it was calm and quiet. He liked to feel the sun on his
face and the earth under his bare feet.

When Johnny turned eighteen, he took a *very* long walk—more than four hundred miles! He brought along food, supplies, and a sack of apple seeds.

Johnny had an idea.

Indiana

Ohio

Settlers were starting to go west in covered wagons, looking for new places to live. Johnny figured they would want apples to eat and press into cider. But there were no apple trees out west. Even if the settlers planted seeds, it would take years for trees to sprout and grow fruit.

Pennsylvania

Why not give the settlers a head start?

Johnny reached Pennsylvania. Near a river, he found a patch of land with rich soil and plenty of sunlight. A perfect place for growing apple trees!

He planted some seeds. Then he built a sturdy
fence so that when the new seedlings came up,
deer and rabbits wouldn't eat them.

It was his first nursery.

Johnny planted more seeds—thousands of them—across Pennsylvania, Ohio, and Indiana. He worked and he walked, going from nursery to nursery to tend his trees.

Meanwhile, the settlers came. Sure enough, they wanted apples! They were happy to pay Johnny a few cents apiece for seedlings. Sometimes he even gave them away to families who were down on their luck.

People spread the word about Johnny and his apple trees. That's how he got his nickname.

Have you met Johnny Appleseed? He's mighty kind, people said. *Mighty peculiar, too!*

It was true. For one thing, Johnny looked strange. He wore old, ragged pants. He cut holes in coffee sacks to make his shirts.

He still didn't wear shoes. By now, folks claimed, his feet were so tough, a snake's fangs couldn't prick them!

People even swore they saw Johnny wear a tin pot for a hat . . .

. . . and then cook his dinner in it!

Johnny's diet was
another thing people
couldn't get over. He
didn't like to hurt
animals, so he wouldn't
eat meat. Not one bite!
He filled up on corn
mush, potatoes, and
nuts instead.

And when night fell, Johnny liked to sleep outdoors. He'd settle into a hollow log or stretch out on a pile of leaves.

He didn't seem to worry about the bears and panthers that roamed the woods. It was almost as if Johnny was a forest creature himself!

Johnny might have been odd, but he was friendly.
He got along with just about everyone he met.

Native Americans shared their trails with him.
They showed him which berries were safe to eat,
and how to make medicine from leaves and roots.

Settlers invited Johnny into their cabins and asked him to tell stories. Sometimes he read from the Bible. "Good news fresh from heaven!" he'd say. Other times, he acted out his own wild adventures.

People retold Johnny's tales . . . and made up new ones, too! As the years went by, the tales grew taller and taller. . . .

Did you know Johnny can thaw ice with his bare feet?

He has a tame wolf that follows him around like a puppy!

Once he tricked ten
woodsmen into a chopping
contest. They cleared a
whole acre of land for
a nursery!

The stories wound their way east and west and back again.

So did Johnny. He traveled hundreds of miles a year, making new nurseries and tending the old ones.

Every so often, he rode a horse or paddled a canoe. But most of the time, he walked. And walked. And walked.

He kept this up for nearly *fifty* years!

One day, when he was seventy years old,
Johnny walked through a snowstorm to fix a
fence around some of his trees. Afterward,
he fell ill and died.

Johnny was sorely missed. But he was not forgotten—
and neither was his great idea.

As settlers moved farther and farther west, they
carried along apple seeds, just the way Johnny had.
They planted apple trees of their own.

Today, apples grow in every state in America!

Johnny and His Apples

The apples that grew on Johnny's trees were mostly "spitters." That meant they were too sour to eat! Settlers used them to make cider and vinegar.

Johnny's worn-out clothes made him look poor, but he wasn't. When he died, he owned over a thousand acres of land.

There's a monument for Johnny in Indiana, near the spot where he died. The stone lists both of his names: JOHN CHAPMAN and JOHNNY APPLESEED. And underneath: HE LIVED FOR OTHERS.

Johnny probably walked more than a hundred thousand miles in his lifetime.